Grandville's Animals

Grandville's Animals

The World's Vaudeville

With an introduction by Bryan Holme

Thames and Hudson

Designed by Christopher Holme

Library of Congress Catalog card number 81-50973
ISBN 0-500-23340-3

Printed in Japan

Introduction

It has been said that if it hadn't been for J. J. Grandville there would have been no John Tenniel and no Edward Lear. And if it hadn't been for the ancient Egyptian mystics who drew animal heads on human bodies, perhaps there would have been no Grandville either.

Grandville's major works were *The Metamorphoses of the Day*, a collection of seventy lithographs published in 1829, and *Scenes from the Private and Public Life of Animals*, published in 1842 with a text by P. J. Stahl (the pseudonym for Pierre-Jules Hetzel, who arranged and published the book) and separate stories by various authors including Honoré de Balzac. It is from these two extraordinary works that the illustrations in this book have been selected; the captions are direct translations from the French.

Nothing like this had been seen before: birds, cats, dogs, elephants, tortoises—even beetles—behaving as well as looking like humans. Adding to the novelty of *Metamorphoses*, which became the rage of Paris, was the new lithography process by which the illustrations were printed.

Clothing his animals in the fashions of the day and giving them human airs, gestures, emotions, and thoughts,

"Woman is gay and playful, visionary and voluptuous, but man is nothing but a reed."

Grandville assigned each of his characters "a role in the world's vaudeville" as Charles Blanc so aptly put it. In familiar settings—the garden, living room, dining room—he brought together the strangest mixture of bedfellows who converse, play, or vie with each other in typical political and domestic situations.

Together with the Grimm brothers' collection of fairytales, which had been published in Germany in 1812 and in England in 1823 under the title of *Household Stories*, Grandville's two books represented milestones in publishing that set the stage for a whole new trend in fairytale and animal story books.

Grandville was to influence hundreds of illustrators. By the 1850s, Charles Bennett had illustrated his bizarre *Aesop's Fables*, a book which could almost be taken for the work of Grandville, and George Cruikshank was drawing Grandvillesque cartoons like his "Fellows of the Zoological Society" for *The Comic Almanack*. In the 1870s, Walter Crane's Beast in *Beauty and the Beast* and Wolf in *Little Red Riding Hood* were in the same Grandville genre. Later came Arthur Rackham, and after the turn of the century, Beatrix Potter, and later still Walt Disney and so very many other young illustrators, each depicting animals as humans in his own particular way. Until recently, however, the far-reaching influence of Grandville's books was never fully recognized outside France except by artists, illustrators, and connoisseurs.

For professional reasons—his father also being an artist—Grandville adopted the stage name of his grandfather, who was an actor of repute. His real name was Jean-Ignace-Isidore Gérard. He was born in Nancy in 1803, briefly attended school there, but soon gave up his studies in order to help his father, who, not untypically for his profession, found it a struggle to make ends meet. In 1823 the family managed to scrape together enough money to send Grandville to Paris, where he was to study art and make his own way. Within a short four years his first illustrations, *Four Seasons of the Human Life*, were published —and shortly thereafter, *Voyage to Eternity*, inspired by Holbein's series of woodcuts *The Dance of Death*.

It has been suggested that Grandville drew much of his inspiration from Pieter Brueghel the Elder, from the fantastic visions of Hieronymous Bosch, and that his style might also possibly have been influenced by Goya, who just then was being "discovered" in Paris. All of this could be true. But Grandville's unique contribution lay not only in his use of animal forms to realize his penetrating insight into human foibles, but also in his ability to discern the humorous characteristics of both humans and animals to the point of finding the two inseparable. Grandville's unerring eye for truth left little room for flattery. Even as a young man, watching his father paint pretty miniatures of his patrons was enough for him to sneak off and somewhat ruthlessly draw the face as it really was. Almost everything Grandville drew became the subject of caricature.

Always politically minded, Grandville fought on the barricades during the rebellion of 1830 which saw the overthrow of Charles X, the last of the Bourbons. Following this, Grandville's artistic talents found a natural outlet in a series of bitingly satirical cartoons commissioned by the journals *Le Charivari* and *Le Caricature.* These cartoons continued to be published until 1835 when Louis-Philippe's government cracked down on the free press. To support himself and his new wife, Margaret, whom he had married in 1833, Grandville turned to the illustration of books, which were to number over twenty-five titles by the time he died in 1847.

Particularly notable among Grandville's other works are editions of La Fontaine's *Fables* and *Gulliver's Travels.* Both of these were published in 1838. *Robinson Crusoe,* the only children's book Grandville illustrated, appeared in 1840 and was followed by *Fables of Florian* in 1842, *Another World* in 1844, and *The Animated Flowers* in 1847. But Grandville will always be best remembered for *Scenes from the Public and Private Life of Animals* and *The Metamorphoses of the Day.*

For the original wood-engraved illustrations for these two works, Hetzel engaged the best wood engravers of the day so full justice would be done to Grandville's designs. In the present book, the colored illustrations have been made from a rare copy of the larger edition, which Pierre-Jules Hetzel also published.

BRYAN HOLME

A cafe

7

The lion of Paris

The debutante

The philosopher and bird of letters

The intrepid student

"In this suit for separation, gentlemen, consider well two things."

"I was chosen by the management for my roar, and that's what I'm doing."

J. J. Grandville

11

"As Machiavelli said: 'The king of a deserted island need have no fear of a revolution.'"

"Surely they're not getting on too?"
"An omnibus, lady, is an omnibus."

The temptation of Minette
"Up here, misery, obscurity;
down there, riches and fame."

A poor little cat, all alone, bewildered . . . an honest reward to the escort who returns her home.

Betrayed again? Is there no end to it?

A natural marriage

A conventional marriage

A marriage of convenience . . . for convenience

"Sir, my respects . . . and my daughter."

Innocence in danger

Mademoiselle Pigoiseau

"In a few years you'll be a big girl, worrying your mother, venturing into the woods where wolves abound."

21

"My wife is out, little pussy cat. Heh! Heh!"

An elopement

23

The doctor's new toy!

"Excuse me, sir, but they told me I'd be certain to find you in at this hour."

Swimming lessons

"Won't you stay and have dinner with us, Mother Pilon?"

*"Atheism, gentlemen, wasn't Maupertius'
only virtue . . . he died of indigestion."*

*Waltzing all winter,
but still putting on weight*

"A permit for hunting? No, that brings bad luck."

29

"I'm well insured . . . and I really couldn't care less."

Dinner at the Club

Off to war

The beetles

"Oh! that horrible man, following us all the time."

"*I am not at home to anybody.*"

THE PLAGIARIST: *like the human magpie who clothes himself in plumes borrowed from others.*

SCHOOLBOY. *Present indicative: I am bored.*
MASTER. *You are bored.*
SCHOOLBOY. *You bore me.*
MASTER. *No, no, not that.*
SCHOOLBOY. *We are bored.*
You bore us.

"I have fifteen million, five castles,
an army of male friends, a regiment of lady friends,
I am considered something of a wit,
but what pleases me most is my modesty."

"You can see,
he turns up the king every time."

"Strait-laced, prudish . . . that's what they are!"

Dog Days

The system of attraction

*An English lady won't say "I love you,"
but she'll willingly sing it.*

Of good breeding, but lesser voice

At the Academy ... so young

The concert

Dancing lesson

In one leap she soars to an immense height.

"If I were a bee, my waistline wouldn't be as slim. I might be admired, but not adored."

A virtuous woman has nothing to hide.

"God! what a remarkable resemblance to you, sir."

"Here you are, my little rats."   "I wish you every happiness, my dearest."

"I did not marry to become a wet nurse . . . and as for you, you wretched little sparrow, lie down at once and go to sleep!"

"Poetry transports me to a dream world ... The earth
fades away ... I float in blue waters ... Be quiet, jackdaws!"

"If I am from the same stock,
I'm certainly not from the same country."

"You have a point there, Gauthier. People who live in beautiful houses aren't necessarily the happiest."

Mr. Martin, the fisherman, brings dinner home for the family.

*"I really don't know. You're not my son;
you're not a blackbird!"*

*"Stick to it,
and finally I'll have my hole."*

The oldest member

55

"The ace of hearts tells me there's clover in your future."

Each takes his pleasure where he finds it.

A single woman daydreams about what?
Of being two?

"Ah! she pleases you, does she now.
You monster!
Well, she's fired!"

"Flunkies . . . am I not the mistress?" *"Of the master, yes!"*

59

Pride and humility

"Mummy, are there really men with faces like that?"

The precious image

Looking at himself in the mirror,
he saw a handsome young man.

"I found the human comedy sufficiently entertaining not to boo—until the final tableau."